I0828405

Monk Parrots

Squawk!

Squawk!

New York City

North America

South America

Monk Parrots

Squawk!

Squawk!

New York City

North America

South America

"I SAW WILD PARROTS IN NEW YORK CITY!"
written George P. Sommers
illustrated by Bill Young

Copyrighted March 2010

ISBN: 978-1-935706-01-4

Library of Congress Control Number: 2010923888

No part of this book may be reproduced or transmitted in any form
or by any means, electronic or mechanical, including photocopying, recording,
or by any information storage and retrieval system,
without permission in writing from the author and publisher.

Wild parrots come from the subtropical and tropical places from around the world, where there are lots of trees to live in and fruit to eat - but.......

……Surprise! Some wild parrots have moved to New York City, where trees can be hard to find – and it's sometimes cold and snowy.

Some say the city parrots were already someone's pets once, like these - and that somehow they got out of their cages and flew out their people's open windows.

Some people think the parrots flew from South America to New York City --- on an airplane and they were supposed to go to pet shops.

I think the container they were in broke open and the parrots flew away to become New Yorkers. ***And I am sticking to my story!***

Monks, sometimes called Quaker parakeets, are native to South America and they live in agricultural regions where they adapt to living amongst humans. Monk parakeets can live in cooler weather because they do something no other kind of parrot does...

They build huge enclosed nests out of sticks. That's their secret for staying warm and dry in the cold New York winters too.

Sometimes LOTS of parrots will have their own apartments in one giant nest.

Since trees are scarce in the city, the parrots sometimes have to build their nests on telephone poles . . .

Mother and father parrots spend much of their day looking for food and the perfect sticks to make home improvements.

The parrots learned from other birds, like this goldfinch, where in the city to find delicious berries and buds - and even free food left by friendly people.

The city pigeons showed the parrots how to find food on the ground, sometimes even breadcrumbs or popcorn!

A lucky parrot might find a garden with a favorite treat - sunflower seeds!

Part of the day has to be set aside to chatter and play, maybe even to find a boy or girl friend.

Instead of using cell phones, they keep in touch all over the city with their loud squawks.

Late in the afternoon, they gather with the flock – their friends and neighbors.

After the sun goes down in New York City, it's time for every Parrot to go to bed to rest up for another busy day!

~ The End ~

Parrots Paparazzi Photography & Ask the Author

Quaker Pair Chatting in New York City

Monk Nest in Tropical Rain Forrest

Closeup of Monk in Native Habitat

Photography by George Sommers ©

Nesting on New York City Telephone Pole.

Monk Nest in Tropical Rain Forrest

Monk Parrot Sleeping in Nest.

Photography by George Sommers ©

George and Pip Enjoying Garden with Giant Sunflowers.

Closeup of Love Birds

Finch on Bird Feeder.

Photography by George Sommers ©

ASK THE AUTHOR
GEORGE SOMMERS ANSWERS CHILDREN'S QUESTIONS

Q. *Is this a true story?*

A. Yes! I visited New York City to write a magazine article about the city's wild parrots, and decided children might enjoy reading about these parrots, too.

Q. *When did you first see parrots in New York?*

A. Right away! Before, I didn't know how hard it would be to see them, or how long it would take. When I first parked my car in a neighborhood where the birds lived, I had music playing on the radio and the air conditioning on because it was a very hot day. Even with all that noise, I heard some squawking, looked out my window and saw two parrots flying over my car.

Q. *What does feral mean?*

A. The NYC parrots are feral. Unlike some birds like blue jays and cardinals, they're not really natives of the United States. They came from South America and were once domesticated – meant to live as pets- but somehow got loose and learned to live in the wild again. Neighbors say the parrots have been in New York City since the 1970s.

Q. *Are there any native American parrots?*

A. The Carolina parakeet was once common in the US, but is now extinct; like the dinosaurs. A kind of Amazon parrot once lived as far north as Arizona and New Mexico.

Q. *What happened to them?*

A. Habitat loss – cutting down forests - took away a lot of their homes. Many Carolina parakeets were killed, sadly, to use their colorful feathers in ladies' hats. Some farmers thought they would steal their crops. Some scientists say Carolina parakeets caught a disease from chickens and many died. American wild areas where the Amazons once lived also have become towns. Hawks like cities because they can find a lot of tasty food like pigeons and squirrels – and occasionally parrots.

Q. *Do parrots make good pets?*

A. Big parrots make big noise – so your neighbors might not be too happy with them. They also make big messes – so whoever cleans your house might not be too happy with them! Many parrots like LOTS of attention, almost like human babies – and that's hard for kids who go to school and have other interests like friends, computers, etc. Parrots cost a lot of money, too. I'd suggest waiting until you're grown up, and doing a lot of research before deciding if a parrot is the right pet for you.

-more-

Q. *Are ANY birds good pets for children?*

A. Parakeets and cockatiels are small members of the parrot family. They can talk and do tricks and are less noisy, messy and expensive than bigger parrots, and they can also entertain themselves when they're alone. Canaries and finches don't talk, but they sing nicely and are easier to take care of.

Q. *Where can I go to see parrots in New York City?*

A. My book's birds live in the Brooklyn neighborhood on the "mid-alphabet" streets of J, K, L, M, etc. and on the Brooklyn College campus. They're very easy to spot in the trees or flying with their bright green coloration and the noise they make! Look for great big nests made out of sticks. They often visit birdfeeders.

Q. *What do I need to watch wild parrots and other birds?*

A. Nothing, except to be where they are: in the city, in the forest, by the seashore - nearly everywhere! You can even watch them right from your window at a birdfeeder in your yard. Lots of birds, like the New York City parrots, aren't very shy.

Eventually, you might want to get a pair of binoculars and a guidebook to help identify birds; or even a camera to take some great photos.

Bird watching is a fun hobby which you can learn a lot from; most importantly how we can protect birds and their homes as precious natural resources. We don't want to see any more birds going extinct like the Carolina parakeet!

Q. *Are there wild parrots anywhere else in America?*

A. Most parrots come from warm, tropical countries and can't live outside in cold and snowy winters. The Quaker, or monk, parrots CAN adapt to the cold, and can be found in many places in the United States.

In some warmer states like Florida, Texas and California other kinds of feral parrots are often found. I have seen parrots while riding down a bicycle path in Siesta Key, Florida and while in line at Universal Studios in California. Cherry headed conures star in the movie "The Wild Parrots of Telegraph Hill" which is available on DVD.

Q. *Are there any other interesting birds that live in the city?*

A. It's not just pigeons in the city! A famous red tail hawk named Pale Male lived in New York's Central Park and had a TV show made about him. Peregrine falcons like to build their homes on cliffs, but skyscrapers work equally well. When they "divebomb" to the ground for food, they are the fastest creatures on earth!

...MORE MONK FACTS

The name monk comes from their grey underside coloration – like that of monks' robes. Some say Quaker comes from sounds they make – or from an occasional "quaking" behavior. Native to Argentina and its neighbors, the adaptable bird lives ferally in much of the US and Europe.

Monks can be trained to talk. Parrots are often credited with having the intelligence (and temperament) of a 2-3 year old human child.

Monk nests, unique among parrots, are constructed with several separate "apartments" for multiple monogamous pairs – and have been recorded weighing up to 90 pounds. Their nests are sometimes considered a nuisance or dangerous in some settings like on baseball fields or on telephone wires – and are sometimes destroyed – but many advocacy groups support legislation to protect the birds, and preservation methods like construction of safe, alternative nesting sites.

Draw or place a picture
of your
favorite bird.

Species of Bird ____________________

Location ___________________________

Date _______________________________

Name ______________________________

GEORGE P. SOMMERS BIOGRAPHY

George P. Sommers is a Long Island, New York native now living in Quincy, Massachusetts with his dear friend Linda Currier, a 20 year old Goffin's cockatoo named Pippy, a cat called Kizmet and some pet fish. He is a graduate of University of Massachusetts at Amherst with a degree in Journalism/English. Mr. Sommers' freelance writing and photography has appeared in international, national and local publications. His articles on pet bird and fish care can currently be viewed in *examiner.com, Boston under PETS,* and in *Clipper Press' "Pet Gazette."*

Special thanks are in order for:

Marc Johnson, who originally tipped the author off about New York City's feral parrots. Mr. Johnson is founder of Foster Parrots, a wonderful organization based in Rhode Island that takes in abandoned parrots and has been instrumental in the preservation and protection of Monk, or Quaker, parrots in their new habitats in New York and several other states. For more information, contact Marc or Karen at marc@fosterparrots.com.

Janelle Barabash of Save our Wild Parrots of New York who gave the author a tour of some of the city's feral parrot hot spots.

The late **Rosa Bova** for inspiring the idea of turning a magazine article into a children's book.

Diana Dell and **Carol Dingle** for their continuing professional support and encouragement.

Linda Currier for her near superhuman patience and understanding.

Rolf Erickson and **Charlie Turner** without whose technical assistance this book would never have been possible.

Learn more @
georgesommers.blogspot.com
wigglespress.com

Monk Parrots

Squawk!

Squawk!

New York City

North America

South America

Monk Parrots

Squawk!

Squawk!

New York City

North America

South America

www.ingramcontent.com/pod-product-compliance
Lightning Source LLC
LaVergne TN
LVHW070204110826
845147LV00002B/495

* 9 7 8 1 9 3 5 7 0 6 0 1 4 *